L. GIUNTA

SAINT PETER'S

VATICAN CITY

ARTISTIC - RELIGIOUS
GUIDE

A. D. MCMLXVIII

NIHIL OBSTAT

A. M. Manzini, Rev. Deleg.

Romae, die 11, februarii 1963

IMPRIMATUR

Aloysius Traglia, Archiep. Caesarien., Vicesgerens

E Vicariatu Urbis

Romae, die 11, februarii 1963

FOREWORD

T he Church, established by Jesus Christ to glorify God and provide man with the means of santification and salvation, has adopted not only the most elevated and symbolic things of creation, but especially the most beautiful art and ideas of great geniuses, offered in gratitude and homage to the Supreme Giver of all material and spiritual good.

This explains the solicitude of the Church, above all in its temples, for architecture, sculpture, painting, music and every form of art. Thus the light of God, which illuminates the human mind is returned to Him in the works of art devoted and consecrated to Him. The great artists have always responded generously to this desire of the Church, and profoundly inspired by these sacred subjects, have placed their genius and art at her disposition, so that their immortal creations may always serve to glorify God, and instil the minds and hearts of the faithful with love, truth and the supreme greatness of God.

Rome, this eternal city of universal life, where the great masters — Michelangelo, Raphael, Bernini and countless other artists — gathered to receive their Baptism of Glory under the generous patronage of the Popes, offers us the sublime vision of the great artists of every epoch, school and style, competing to create a temple of inimitable splendour, beautifying it with their art, and effecting therein a veritable artistic and religious *teaching, presenting in every image and picture an affirmation of the love of religion.*

The object of this guide, which I have sought to make concise, clear in exposition and rich in illustration, is to show what the mind can produce when illuminated and inspired by religion, it is also an address to the mind of the visitor to lead him, by the admiration of these works of art, to the knowledge of the sacred teaching of religion and to God.

Hence, I present an Artistic-Religious Guide.

L. G

The numbers in round brackets refer to the plan, those in square brackets to the notes at the end of the book.

The dotted line with arrows in the plan indicates the route for a complete tour of the Basilica.

Photos: *Alinari - Anderson - Giordani - Chauffourier - Luchi - Sansaini.*

THE TOMB OF ST. PETER

T he Apostles, having received the Holy Ghost, spread throughout the world to preach the gospel of their Divine Master. Peter their head, came to Rome, Capital of the Roman Empire, to found there the church of Christ, and to establish the center of Christianity. Here he continued the work of Redemption begun by the Saviour. Here he endured discomforts, privations and sacrifices. Here he suffered in the dark and damp Mamertine prison. About the year 65 on the slopes of the Vatican, he sealed his apostolate with the sacrifice of his life on a rough and heavy cross, which he requested be placed upside down, since he did not consider himself worthy of imitating his Master in His martyrdom. After the guards had left, some faithful followers, who in tears had assisted at the Crucifixion of Peter, buried the lifeless body of the martyr beside the Northern wall of the Circus of Nero, near a small Pagan cemetery.

Pope St. Clement only a few years after the death of Peter wrote to the Corinthians « ... St. Peter bore numerous tribulations, he underwent martyrdom and has proceeded to the eternal resting place which awaited him. »

On the spot where the First Apostle had been buried, St. Anacletus, his third successor, built a small oratory « *Memoria Sancti Petri* », near which the Popes of the early centuries were buried, according to their expressed request.

Nero passed away, as did all the other cruel persecutors of the followers of Christ, but the memory of Peter remained alive among the Christians of Rome. That cradle of primitive Christianity, that small apostolic tomb, which was to become the object of universal veneration, for more than two centuries received the tears and heard the prayers of the first converts who asked the great martyr for his faith and his courage to endure with fortitude their certain and not far off martyrdom.

When the persecutions ceased, the Emperor Constantine, by the Edict of Milan in the year 313, gave freedom to the Church. Following the advice of Pope St. Sylvester, he also proposed to build a sumptuous basilica over the tomb of St. Peter, where the small oratory of Anacletus stood. It was begun in 324 and consecrated November 18, 326, by Pope Sylvester.

Tradition has it that the Emperor himself had twelve baskets of earth transported from the Holy Land in memory of the twelve Apostles, which he personally placed in the foundations.

The *Liber Pontificalis* describes the verification of the tomb of the great apostle, which was made in the presence of the Pope and the Emperor. The sacred remains of the Apostle were put under the central altar in a precious gilt bronze sarcophagus surmounted by a golden cross.

THE CONSTANTINE BASILICA

I n shape it was not very different from the present Basilica of St. Paul on the Via Ostiense. By 35 marble stairs from the square « *Cortina Sancti Petri* » one entered a large terrace where the Emperors and Sovereigns, who used to pay homage to the tomb of the humble fisherman of Galilee, were received by the clergy.

This custom still exists. When an Ambassador (or representative of the head of a State or Government) after presenting his credentials to the Holy Father, goes down into the Basilica in front of the main door, he is received by four canons of the Chapter of St. Peter in choir dress, and is accompanied on the visits which he makes to the altars of the Blessed Sacrament, of the Madonna, also called Gregorian, and the Tomb of St. Peter.

To the right of the terrace there was a beautiful romanesque bell-tower built in 752 by Pope Stephen II. Three doors led into a large four-portico court-yard, 183.72 ft. wide and 203.39 ft. long, supported by 46 columns. In the center, amidst flower beds and plants, there stood a lovely monument called the « *Cantharus* » adorned by a large bronze pinecone « *Pigna* », which is still kept in one of the Vatican courtyards, named after it. It was surrounded by eight porphyry columns decorated with two bronze peacocks and four gilt dolphins. The walls were decorated with frescoes, representing the lives of the Apostles and lined with artistic mausoleums of Popes and sovereigns who deemed it an honor to lie near the tomb of St. Peter.

This atrium was used for the meetings of penitents or catechumens who were not allowed to take part in the divine rites, also to serve food to the

Fig. 1. - The Facade of Constantine Basilica.

needy, or even as a place were the poor begged alms and where pilgrims could rest, etc.

The facade had six large windows and was decorated with mosaic representing Christ and the four Evangelists together with the relative symbolic animals, and the emperor Constantine in an attitude of prayer. (fig. 1).

There were five entrances to the church, the central one of which was called the silver door because it was artistically worked in laminated silver, and these led to five naves, 387 ft. long and 210,8 wide, divided by 88 columns arranged in four rows of 22 columns each.

In the presbytery, under a canopy supported by four columns of porphyry, stood the papal altar which had been erected over St. Peter's tomb, thus the Holy Sacrifice was offered directly over the sepulchre of the Apostle. This presbytery was approached by two lateral staircases running along the wall, in which was a silver window called the « Fenestella Confessionis » through which the tomb of St. Peter could be seen and touched with religious articles.

The rare value of the marbles, the columns, the paintings, the mosaics which beautified the walls, the impressive balustrade, the sumptuous sepulchres which through centuries were placed along the walls; the 120 altars, 27 of which were dedicated to the Blessed Virgin under different titles, rich in rare marble and gilt, mosaics, frescoes, bas-reliefs and statues, the scenes and designs of the 72 stained glass windows, the many delicate ciboriums rich in miniatures and precious stones, the artistic bronze valves, the monumental private chapels belonging to the most famous Roman families such as, the Orsini, the Stefaneschi, the Pallavicini, the Tebaldeschi, the Cesarini and many others, the artistic oratories next to the Church, the wealth and abundance of the lamps, all made it a really grandiose temple, in which every century left a profound trace of its art and devotion. (fig. 2)

It received the artistic homage of every age, from Constantine to Charlemagne; of all styles from the lively Byzantine to the strong Romanesque, from the severe Gothic to the elegant Renaissance; of all of the artists from Cavallino to Giotto, from Arnolfo da Cambio to Mino da Fiesole, Donatello, Filarete, and Pollaiolo. At the same time, all the Popes and those nations enlightened by Christianity enriched it with their gifts and donations.

HISTORY OF THE NEW BASILICA

Unfortunately the original Constantine Basilica, which had been the goal of pilgrimages of the whole Christian world for twelve centuries, was reduced to such a state of ruin that it threatened to collapse. This was in part due to the wear and tear of time and the instability of the foundations which were based on the ruins of Nero's Circus.

Nicholas V, the first humanist Pope, decided to reconstruct the old temple, and in 1452 entrusted the task to Leon Battista Alberti who with the help of Bernardo Rossellino began to build a new and larger apse for the church.

The work, however, proceeded very slowly and there was very little progress made under Pope Paul II and his architect, Giuliano da San Gallo, whom he had employed in 1470.

Credit for having put an end to all delay belongs to Julius II, a Pope of strong and energetic character. He proposed to build over the remains of the Prince of the Apostles the most wonderful temple that the human mind could conceive and the effort of man could accomplish; a magnificent temple, artistic and imposing which would also be a real expression of the greatness and beauty of the faith and the Church.

The task of demolition and reconstruction was entrusted to Bramante, an eminent architect and a recognized student of classical Romanism. He designed the temple in the form of a Greek cross with towers, columns and

Fig. 2. - The Interior of Constantine Basilica.

small domes, dominated by a huge central dome on a square base. He was known to say: « I will take the vaults of the Pantheon, and I will build them onto the arches of the Basilica of Massenzio. »

On April 18, 1506, the Pope in person laid the first stone on the spot wich to-day corresponds with the Pillar of Veronica. Then Bramante began to pull down a large part of the building leaving only the front part of the ancient Church. For this demolition work he was named « Mastro Ruinante » (Master Destroyer).

With the death of Julius II on February 21, 1513, followed by that of Bramante thirteen years later, construction work remained almost at a standstill. Little progress was made for two reasons: artists called upon to direct the work, Raffaello Sanzio and the aged Giuliano da San Gallo with his nephew Antonio, wanted to bring about substantial modifications and transformations in the Bramante project; the tragic Sack of Rome in 1527 when the Barbaric hordes pillaged churches, convents and palaces, spreading desolation and misery in the city of the Popes.

After the death of Antonio da San Gallo, Pope Paul III (Farnese) turned to Michelangelo. He was perhaps the only artist who, with his growing fame and recognized genius, could bring to an end the continuous changing of designs and projects and complete the formidable undertaking. Although seventy two years of age and recuperating from a serious illness he accepted the arduous task, in his own words « for the love of God and veneration of the Prince of the Apostles ». This was to be done without payment, but on the sole condition that he might exercise unlimited powers in the direction of the work. This condition was not only accepted by the Pope but was sanctioned on January 1, 1547, by a Papal Brief in which the great artist was appointed chief architect of the Basilica with the liberty to change, renew, extend, and restrict *(immutandi, reformandi, ampliandi et restringendi)* at his own discretion.

Excluding the various projects of the past, Michelangelo kept close to that of Bramante, only modifying and simplifying it, but making it greater, more linear and more beautiful. He gave the greatest emphasis to the dome; a dome which is not that of the Pantheon, nor that of Bramante or San Gallo, but a completely new creation worthy of the titanic genius of the great architect; a dome of a design so simple and at the same time so grand, harmonious, powerful and noble that the human mind had never before been able to visualize.

Based on a huge travertine construction and consisting of massive pillars in rhythmic formation, of windows, niches and lodges opening up and giving the whole an appearance of elegantly curved lines, this dome rises in an upward trend of power, beauty and sublimity like a hymn of glory to the Greatness and Majesty of God. (fig. 3).

The tireless work of the wonderful old artist continued for sixteen years, during which time a great deal more was achieved than in the proceding ninety-five years. The dome was built as far as the drum, the three arms of the Church were constructed, the Gregorian Chapel completed and the inside and outside of the temple was decorated with elegant reinforced pillars. The rich Corinthian capitals ornamenting these pillars were one of the most pleasing creations of Michelangelo's genius.

The great master, being very advanced in years, foresaw that he would not be able to see his work completed, and fearing that his successors might alter his plan he worked for four years on a model in wood which would serve as a pattern for those who were to continue with his project.

After the death of Michelangelo on February 18, 1564, the direction of the work was given to Pirro Ligorio and Giacomo Vignola. The former was immediately dismissed because he wanted to alter the design of the deceased architect, while the second continued the construction and completed two lateral domes.

At least twenty-four years had passed since the death of Michelangelo and no one had dared to set about the completion of the immense main dome until the intrepid and energetic Sixtus V. giving orders to finish the work whatever the cost and in the shortest time possible, entrusted the difficult undertaking to Giacomo della Porta and Domenico Fontana, the latter being already famous for the erection of the Vatican Obelisk.

The two architects at once set about their arduous task. With a colossal

Fig. 3. - The Basilica seen from the Vatican Gardens.

scaffolding requiring 15,000 quintals of hemp (quintal = 220 lbs), 10,000 quintals of iron and 100,000 beams, as well as with the untiring efforts of 800 workmen who with the light of torches worked even during the night, they completed the work. Thus the great Pope, twenty-two months later had the great satisfaction of admiring from the Quirinal Palace, where he lived the most gigantic work of the Renaissance. Since that day the dome of the most august Church of Christendom, synthesis of strength and beauty, climbs up with its olympic structure into the sky of Rome to which it has become a necessary complement and a symbol representing the sign, the seal, the heraldic emblem of Christianity.

The great project of Michelangelo would have been almost completely executed if Paul V in 1605 had not intervened. Being of the opinion that the temple was too small and not exactly suited to the requirements of the liturgy, he decided to transform the temple into a Latin cross, prolonging the eastern arm by three arches.

Among the many projects presented, that of Maderno was chosen. He directed the demolition work of the remains of the old temple, and then the reconstruction of the new Church and facade. On November 18, 1626, thirteen centuries after the consecration of the Constantine Basilica, Urban VIII solemnly consecrated the new Basilica.

From the beginning of the work, under the Pontificate of Nicholas V, to its completion, one hundred and seventy-four years had passed, and twenty Popes had sat on the throne of St. Peter.

The construction of the Basilica had been completed; now it was necessary to consider decorating and beautifying it.

Julius II and Paul III had found in Bramante and Michelangelo architectural geniuses. Urban VIII discovered in Gian Lorenzo Bernini the artist who embellished, animated and put life into that immense space with its huge coloured marbles, statues, columns, niches between the pillars and elegant lodges which break up the monotony of the walls and give light and movement to the greatest temple of Christianity.

Pope Urban VIII, a great patron of art, on meeting Bernini, the artist with so versatile a mind and so vivid an imagination, made a remark which has remained famous in history : « It is a great fortune, Cavaliere, to see Cardinal Maffeo Barberini as Pope, but it is still more fortunate for us that Cavaliere Bernini lives in our Pontificate ».

Immediately after Maderno's death, Bernini was appointed architect of the Basilica and for more than fifty years, with really prodigious and creative talent he beautified and enriched it with those works of art which we shall admire later. After the construction and decoration, various sepulchral monuments of which we shall speak later were added to the Basilica. They show the evolution of sculpture from the time of the Renaissance, connected with such names as Pollaiolo, Bernini, della Porta, Algardi, Rusconi, Canova, Thorwaldsen and others.

In order to cover the cold bareness of the walls and vaults, another element used was mosaic, rightly called « the painting of eternity ». With its scintillating variety of colours, it covered the domes, the supports of the dome, the lunettes, and even surrounded the altar pictures, some of which were copied from the masterpieces of such great painters as Raphael, Domenichino, Guercino, Reni.

The sculpture in St. Peter's did not stop with the papal sepulchres, but continued with the erection of statues to the founders of the religious orders as they were canonized.

All that the magnificent architecture of the great temple now lacked was the sacristy. It was to the merit of Pope Pius VI and the architect Carlo Marchionni that in 1784 a beautiful, and rich marble sacristy, worthy of the Vatican Basilica, was added.

Fig. 4. - St. Peter's Square.

A VISIT TO THE BASILICA

ST PETER'S SQUARE (fig. 4): Let us pause for a few minutes at the end of the Square and look towards the facade of the Basilica. The visitor's glance is immediately struck by the immensity of MICHELANGELO'S DOME. The great artist has given to the architectural lines an upward movement which provides the main attraction of the Church.

The entire Church gives the appearance of being the only pedestal worthy of this immense Dome with its gracious purity of curve reaching into the sky high above Rome symbolizing the faith in Christ which dominates Humanity. The immense monumental square with its magnificent proportions does not immediately impress the visitor with its true greatness and vastness.

Note the smallnes of the figures of people near the facade. Also consider that the diameter of its eight columns is 9.08 ft. and that the globe of the dome which has a diameter of 8.20 ft. can hold 16 persons.

The square was designed and built by Bernini during the Pontificate of Alexander VII. The front part with its elliptical shape reminds us of the Flavian amphitheatre (the Colosseum) only much larger. It is enclosed by an imposing travertine colonnade, inspired by Greek-Roman art, formed by 284 columns arranged in four rows, making three corridors amidst a forest of columns. (fig. 5).

Above the colonnade there is a rich entablature crowned by a beautiful balustrade on which the statues of 140 Saints are arranged. The ingenuous construction of this colonnade is based on three criteria, namely: Sentimental, in so far as it reconstructs a motive for the Paleo-Christian art; Aestetic, by giving to the square the most beautiful and successful arrangement that the human genius could imagine; Symbolic, by portraying two huge arms of the true Church of Jesus Christ, embracing in a gesture of love all those who hope and believe in Her.

At the sides of the obelisk, which forms the gnomon to the sundial indicated within the area of the square, are TWO BEAUTIFUL FOUNTAINS from which water gushes forming lovely plumes in which sometimes the colours of the rainbow can be seen. These fountains with their high silver spray and their water falling into large pools add a note of freshness and joyfulness to the normal solemnity of the square. On the right stands the older of the two, having been transferred there by Alexander VII, while the other was erected for symmetry by Clement X. (fig. 6).

On the right facing the Basilica, are the massive VATICAN PALACES. As the eye of the pilgrim searches among the many windows of the top floor it rests on the third from the right, which is the window of the room in which the Holy Father lives, prays and works for Christianity. Through it, beyond the ancient walls, he seems to hear the beating of the great heart of our Common Father.

On each side between the fountain and the obelisk there is a disk of green porphyry. From this point, which is the center of the semi-circle, as you look towards the colonnade, instead of the four rows of columns, you can see only one row.

In the center of the square, rising to a height of 137.79 ft., high and majestic, stands the oriental OBELISK of red granite which seems to defy the centuries. The Emperor Caius Caligola had it transported from the Sun Temple of Heliopolis in Egypt to adorn his Circus, later named Neronian after the Emperor who enlarged it.

14

Fig. 5. - Detail of the Colonnade.

In 1586 Pope Sixtus V appointed Domenico Fontana to direct the work of its removal from the Circus, and its erection on the spot where it now stands. (fig. 7). The difficult task was accomplished after fifty-two attempts by the use of five very strong levers, fortyseven capstans, one-hundred and forty horses and nine-hundred men. If one considers the limited means of the times, it now seems almost legendary. On September 10, 1586, during the last and successful attempt, the chronicles of the time narrate that all Rome was present in the square. It is said, but without any historical foundation, that during the difficult operation a sailor, named Bresca from San Remo, hearing the ropes creak, (against the wishes of the Pope who ordered those present to observe perfect silence), cried out in a loud voice: « Water for the ropes ». He not only was not punished, but was rewarded with the privilege, which still belongs to his descendants, of providing the Basilica with palms during Holy Week.

On September 27, 1586, the Pope solemnly blessed the Obelisk, crowning it with a cross. In 1730, Innocent XIII had a relic of the True Cross

Fig. 6. - One of the fountains.

enclosed in it so that any believer coming to the tomb of St. Peter might be able to worship it as a symbol of religion triumphing over a pagan monument.

The following inscriptions are carved into the base on one side: « *Ecce Crux Domini, Fugite partes adversae, vicit leo de tribu Judae* ». (Behold, the Cross of the Lord, begone, ye enemies, the lion of the tribe of Judah has conquered). And on the opposite side: « *Christus vincit, Christus regnat, Christus imperat, Christus ab omni malo plebem suam defendat* ». (Christ conquers, Christ reigns, Christ rules, May Christ defend his people from all evil).

As a silent witness, this obelisk assisted the gladiators at the games, the orgies and fights amongst the crowds, blood-thirsty and drunk with pleasure. It greeted the appearance of the Cross in the eternal city of the Caesars, a sign of humiliation for the pagans and of triumph and salvation for the followers of Christ. It later saw this sign of contradiction turned upside down to receive, midst unspeakable tortures, the worn out members of the first Apostle. Reddened by the blood of martyrs, it also saw them torn to pieces by beasts, submitted to the most cruel and inhuman torments, consumed by flames as they were attached like torches to the trees of the surrounding gardens. After having seen the persecutors of Christ and of the Church pass one by one, it has now become the pedestal of the Cross of Christ and a symbol of the rock-like solidity of the faith which has triumphed during the centuries. It sees the exaltation of the martyrs to the highest honours. It assists at the triumph of the religion of Christ and of His Vicar when it is surrounded by seas of people gathered to listen to the message of the Pope and to receive his blessing. It listens to the prayers and hymns of the faithful who come from all parts of the world to the Eternal City to venerate the sepulchre of St. Peter. (fig. 8).

THE FACADE is by Carlo Maderno who worked on it from 1607 to 1614. The lack of proportion between the length, 385.15 ft., and the height 149.27 ft., of the facade, is immediately noticeable, although remarkable for its power and greatness, this is the reason why it seems at the same time heavy and monotonous. In excusing the artist, one must note that he could not have developed it in height since this would have hidden the view of the Dome, and also, that at the sides where the two clocks designed by Valadier are, there should have been two beautiful towers, according to the plan of Maderno. No doubt these towers would have made it more varied and slender, but when they ried and slender, but they had to be discontinued because the foundations were unsound.

Beneath the clock on the left are the bells, the largest of which has a circumference of

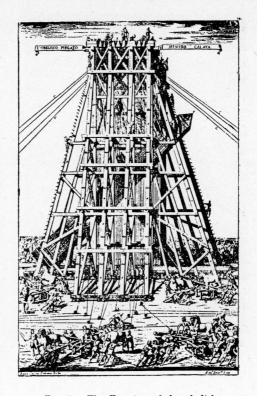

Fig. 7. - The Erection of the obelisk.

24.60 ft. and weighs about 10 tons. The coat of arms on the tympanum of the triangular pediment is that of Paolo Camillo Borghese whose name is included in the inscription: « *In honorem Principis Apostolorum Paulus Burghesius Romanus Pontifex Maximus Anno MDCXII Pontificatus VII* ».

From the central balcony of the facade, the first Cardinal of the Order of Deacons leans out to proclaim to the huge crowd gathered in the square and to the Catholic world the name of the newly elected Pope: « *Nuntio vobis gaudium magnum, habemus Pontificem* ». « I announce to you a great joy, we have a Pope ». In Easter Sunday and on other occasions, the Pope appears on the balcony to speak to the people and give his blessing.

The thirteen statues on the top of the balustrade, 18.70 ft. high, represent the Redeemer, St. John the Baptist and eleven of the Apostles. The statues of St. Peter and St. Paul stand at the foot of the approach like two

Fig. 8. - S. Peter's square (Nat. Pilgrimage of Ital. Cath. Youth.)

divine keepers guarding the Basilica. The bas-relief below the balcony, representing Jesus Christ giving the keys to St. Peter, is by Buonvicino.

THE PORTICO (fig. 9): designed by Maderno, has five beautiful iron gates. *(1)*. With its perfect proportions, its pure and harmonious lines, its rich decorations in ancient gold on the white background of the vault decorated with 32 statues depicting the first Popes, who died martyrs for the faith, its medallions representing episodes from the Acts of the Apostles, its precious and ancient columns adorning the entrances, its imposing pillars in severe yet elegant Doric, all combine to make it the masterpiece of the artist from Bissone, and a worthy vestibule to the greatest temple of the world. *(2)*. The slabs of white marble placed inside the central gate bear the names of the dignitaries of the Church present at the solemn proclamation of the dogma of the Assumption of Our Lady made by Pope Pius XII on November 1, 1950.

At the sides there are equestrian statues of two great defenders of the Church like two sentinels on guard at the tomb of St. Peter.

Fig. 9. -The Portico (on the right: the Holy Door, at the end: Charlemagne's statue)

On the right, behind the great gate leading to the Vatican Palaces, there is the STATUE OF CONSTANTINE. *(3)*. The great Emperor is caught at the dramatic moment when he saw in the heavens the Cross with the words « *In hoc signo vinces* » « In this sign thou shalt conquer », the omen of victory in the decisive battle against Massentius. The marvellous group, full of life, set in front of a curtain which seems to be blown away by a very strong wind, is one of the most beautiful works of the great artist. It was ordered by Innocent X in 1654 and completed under Clement X, 16 years later. (fig. 10).

The statue on the opposite side represents CHARLEMAGNE, *(4)* founder of the Holy Roman Empire and great defender of the rights of the Church, who, at Christmas 799 in this Basilica, after attending midnight mass with his two sons, was crowned by Pope Leo III. The statue is the work of Agostino Cornacchini (1725) and has a lovely mosaic background set off by valuable columns of ancient marble and a curtain of Siena yellow.

Corresponding with the gates of the portico there are five doors to the Basilica. The central door of bronze, *(5)* commissioned by Eugene IX in

Fig. 10. - Statue of Constantine *(Bernini)*

1433 is the work of the Florentine Antonino Averulino, (Filarete). It is divided into six unequal panels, and framed by a rich freize of acanthus' leaves interwoven with figures, animals, classical heads, imperial medallions and mythological scenes. (fig. 11).

On the top left panel of the door is the « Saviour of the World », in the middle, St. Paul with the symbolic flowered vase; underneath, the martyrdom of the Apostle, his condemnation and beheading, and his appearance to the matron Plautilla to return to her the veil which she had used to cover his eyes.

On the top right panel of the door is the Blessed Virgin; in the middle, St. Peter delivering the keys to the kneeling Pope Eugene IV; below, the Crucifixion of St. Peter in the presence of Nero and the Tiber flowing tortuously amongst the main monuments of Pagan Rome: the Pyramid of Caius Cestus, Hadrian's Mausoleum and the Sepulchre of Scipio.

The bas-relief over the door, attributed to Bernini, represents Jesus entrusting His flock to St. Peter; « *Pasce agnos meos* », « Feed my sheep ».

The last door on the right, is the Holy Door. *(6)*. It is solemnly opened by the Pope every 25 years at the proclamation of the Jubilee year and all

20

Fig. 11. - The central door.

Fig. 12. - « The Navicella » (St. Peter's bark - *Giotto)*

the faithful entering into the Church by this door and saying the prescribed prayers gain a Plenary Indulgence. The last Holy Year was proclaimed in 1950 when great crowds of pilgrims came from all parts of the Catholic world.

On the opposite side and above the main entrance to the portico, although unfortunately in an unfavourable light, one can see the famous mosaic called the « NAVICELLA » by Giotto *(7)* ordered by Cardinal Stefaneschi, Canon of the Basilica, in 1298 for the great Jubilee of 1300 (fig. 12). The cardinal is portrayed as the figure which rises from the waves on Christ's left. The scene is taken from the Gospel of St. Matthew: Jesus, walking on the sea, meets the Apostles in a boat tossed by the waves, and stretches out an encouraging hand to Peter who, in a gesture of faith, having seen his Teacher from afar, throws himself into the stormy sea to meet him, while his companions watch the scene with varying expressions of terror and amazement.

This mosaic was originally placed in the atrium of the Constantine Basilica and after many removals and unfortunate restorations, it was placed in its present location. [1].

Fig. 13. - Interior of the Basilica.

VISIT TO THE INTERIOR OF THE BASILICA — GENERAL VIEW: The dimensions of the Basilica appear at first sight much smaller than they really are, the perfect harmony of the various parts gives one this impression. « In St. Peter's », writes Goethe, « I learnt to understand that art as well as nature can render any comparison useless ». (fig. 13).

The grandeur unique in the world, the colossal dimensions, become evident when we examine some of the details. Notice, for example, the angels of the artistic holy water fonts. *(8)*. From a distance they seem to be quite normal in size but if they were erect they would be more than 7 ft. high. (fig. 14).

The central nave which is a combination of Michelangelo's design and Maderno's addition, is separated from the aisles by 8 colossal pillars. These pillars are crowned with rich Corinthian capitals which support the arches leading to the side chapels. In the corners of these arches there are placed 28 figures, 16.40 ft. high, representing the Virtues; while in the niches between the pillars are statues of Saints who founded religious orders.

23

They are:

entering on the right:
below: St. Theresa, F. Valle;
above: St. Madeleine Barat, E. Quattrini;
below: St. Vincent de Paul, P. Bracci;
above: St. John Eudes, S. Silva;
below: St. Philip Neri, G. B. Maini;
above: St. John B. de la Salle, C. Aureli;
above: St. John Bosco, P. Canonica.

On the left:
below: St. Peter of Alcantara, F. Vergara;
above: St. Lucy Filippini, S. Silva;
below: St. Camillus of Lellis, P. Pacilli;
above: St. L. M. Grignion de Montfort, E. Parisini;
below: St. Ignatius of Loyola, G. Rusconi;
above: St. Anthony M.Zaccaria, C. Aureli;
below: St. Francis of Paola, G. B. Maini;
above: St. Peter Fourier, C. Adamos.

Over the architraves of the central nave, on a golden background appear the following words addressed to St. Peter by Jesus Christ: « *Quodcumque ligaveris super terram, erit ligatum et in coelis. Et quodcumque solveris super terram erit solutum et in coelis. Ego rogavi pro te, o Petre, ut non deficiat fides tua et tu aliquando conversus confirma fratres tuos.* (Whatsoever thou shalt bind upon earth shall be bound also in Heaven and whatsoever thou shalt loose on earth, shall be loosed also in Heaven. I have prayed for thee, o Peter, that thy faith fail not and thou, being converted, confirm thy brethren).

The sides of the pillars are decorated with 40 medallions, in multi-coloured marble, of the first 40 Popes raised to the honours of the altar, alternated with the emblems of the tiara and the keys gracefully supported by winged angels, and, at the ends, the dove of the Pamphylian emblem, belonging to Innocent X. Besides the central dome, there are 10 smaller ones, 4 of them circular, surrounding the main dome, and 6 elliptical, (3 on each side aisle) all with mosaic decorations describing religious motives referring to the respective Chapels.

Fig. 14. - Holy water font.

Over the three doors of the central nave there are large inscriptions. The middle one records the lengthening of the Basilica under Pope Paul V; the one on the right, the decorations and donations of Innocent X; that on the left, the consecration of the Basilica by Pope Urban VIII, 18 November 1625. The great red Egyptian porphyry disk in one of the six, which decorated the floor of the ancient Basilica. *(9)*. Twenty three Emperors, from Charlemagne to Frederick III, knelt on this as they were crowned, and no one was allowed to walk over it.

To show that this Basilica, 632 ft. long, is the longest in the world, the measurements of the most important churches are indicated on the floor (10). St. Paul's, London - 520 ft.; S. Maria del Fiore in Florence - 485.48 ft.; Milan Cathedral - 459 ft.;

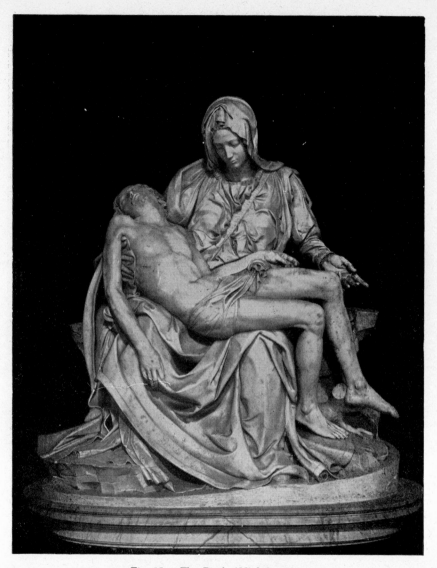

Fig. 15. - The Pietà (*Michelangelo*).

Fig. 16. - The blessed Virgin · Pietà *(Michelangolo)*

Fig. 17. - Detail of the Pietà *(Michelangelo)*

Rheims Cathedral - 455 ft. The Basilica can hold about 80,000 people and covers an area of 49,733 sq. ft.

In St. Peter's there are 597 columns, 100 large marble statues, 160 travertine statues, 90 in stucco and 40 in bronze, 44 altars and 290 windows.

VISIT IN DETAIL: Having taken a general glance at the Basilica, let us take a closer view to observe one by one the art treasures that enrich it. Beginning from the right, we find ourselves in front of the most precious jewel of the temple:

THE PIETA' OF MICHELANGELO. *(11)* (fig. 15-16-17). This famous group which the great artist made when he was only twenty-four. was originally in the Chapel of the Kings of France where it adorned the tomb of Cardinal Jean de Villiers who ordered it from the young sculptor in 1498. It is the only work which bears the artist's name, which we can see written on the facing of Our Lady's garment: « *Michael Angelus Bonarotus florent. faciebat* ». The great sculptor did this in order to dispel the doubts of the many envious people who did not want to believe it to be his own work, but attributed it to Cristoforo Solari.

Fig. 18 - The martyrdom of St. Sebastian
(Domenichino)

This masterpiece of Christian sculpture is the most moving work of the divine artist. The Virgin Mother, beautiful in her pure youth, filled with intense sadness and a profound yet resigned and composed sorrow, leans, full of pity, over the lifeless body of her son lying in tender abandonment on her lap.

When it was pointed out to the great Master that the Madonna seemed too young, he replied, that in this way he wanted to express the incorruptible purity of the Mother of God; and, one day, speaking to his pupil Condivi, he told him that he tried to express on the Virgin's face the certainty of the Resurrection of her Son, besides that the resigned sorrow.

The painting in the vault depicts the triumph of the Cross, whose base, held up by Angels, seems always turned towards the observer.

The spiral column to the right is one of the twelve, which stood in the ancient Basilica and are believed to have come from the temple of Jerusalem. [2].

The HOLY DOOR recently made in bronze is to the right. ST. PETER, a mosaic by G. Calandra, stands over the door.

MONUMENT OF LEO XII (*12 - a little further on*) by De Fabriis, shows him giving the blessing during the Holy Year 1825. CHAPEL OF THE RELICS (*13*) so called because of the number of relics of Saints kept here [3]. At the back there is an ancient wooden Crucifix, attributed to Pietro Cavallini. In the middle of the Chapel there is a lift which communicates with

Fig. 19. - Monument of Innocent XII.

the Pauline Chapel in the Vatican Palaces, which the Holy Father uses to go to the Basilica.

MONUMENT OF QUEEN CHRISTINE OF SWEDEN *(14 - opposite)* who died in 1689 in Rome, and was buried in the Vatican crypt. The bas-relief on the urn, sculptured by Giovanni Teudon, represents the abjuration of Protestantism made by the Queen at Innsbruck, November 3, 1655.

CHAPEL OF ST. SEBASTIAN. *(15)*. Captain of the first Cohort of the Pretorians, who under Emperor Diocletian was bound to a tree on the Palatine Hill and martyred by arrows because he had been converted to Christianity. (fig. 18). The bright mosaic, full of life and movement, was copied in 1738 from the fresco of Domenichino which is in the Church of St. Maria degli Angeli.

MONUMENT OF PIUS XI *(16 - on the right)*, by Canonica. The great

29

Fig. 20 - Monument of Countess Matilda of
Canossa *(Bernini)*

Pope of the Conciliation and of Catholic Action, predecessor of Pius XII happily reigning.

MONUMENT OF INNOCENT XII (17), who died in 1700, is in the passage to the next Chapel. (fig. .18). The group shows the Pope in the act of blessing and on either side Charity with a cherub at her feet and another in her arms; and Justice, with sword and scales.

MONUMENT OF COUNTESS MATILDA OF CANOSSA *(18-opposite)* by Bernini, 1635. (fig. 19). The noble and majestic figure of the famous protectress of the Pope, with her face expressing both classical beauty and strenght of character carries in her left hand the Tiara and Keys and in her right the staff of Command, to show the authority used by her in defense of the Papacy. The bas-relief on the urn, represents the scene which took place in January 1077 at the Castle of Canossa when Henry IV, Emperor of Germany, in hair shirt and ashes, knelt at the feet of the indomitable Gregory VII to be freed from excommunication.

THE BLESSED SACRAMENT CHAPEL *(19)* is entered through a magnificent iron gate designed by Borromini. (fig. 20). After saying a

Fig. 21 - The blessed Sacrament Chapel.

prayer to Jesus, ever present in the Eucharist, we can observe the rich and gorgeous decorations of twenty-nine bas-reliefs by Giacomo Perugini representing symbols and figures from Holy Scripture.

The very rich TABERNACLE, in which the Sacred Host is kept, is one of the most beautiful works of Bernini, ordered in 1674 by Clement X whose coat of arms stands out at the sides of the Altar. It is a small scale copy of the Little Temple of Bramante which is to be found at St. Peter in Montorio. It is surrounded by twelve small Corinthian columns, overlayed with lapis-lazuli and crowned with the statues of the twelve Apostles. The statue of the Divine Redeemer is on the Dome. On either side, two very beautiful

Fig. 22 - Monument of Gregory XIII (*C. Rusconi*)

Fig. 23 - Last Communion of St. Jerome (*Domenichino*)

Angels in gilt bronze with their hands clasped together in profound worship, seem to invite the faithful to join with them in rendering devout homage of faith and love to Jesus ever present in the Eucharist. [4]. The picture behind the altar portraying the Holy Trinity is by Pietro da Cortona.

ALTAR OF ST. FRANCIS OF ASSISI *(20-on the right)* depicted receiving the Holy Stigmata, copied from a picture by Domenichino, is on the right. The two columns at the side, together with that of the Chapel of the Pietà, are from the Constantine Temple. To the left, one of the Basilica's five organs.

MONUMENT OF GREGORY XIII *(21-in the next passage)* by Camillo Rusconi, (fig. 21). The Pope, in the act of giving his blessing, is seated majestically on the sarcophagous, uncovered by Strength with shield and helmet revealing the bas-relief depicting the event which immortalized this Pope: « The Reform of the Calendar of Julius Caesar ». As a reult of this reform, the year 1584 was shortened by ten days, from 4 to 15 October. To the left: the figure of Religion looking with admiration at the Pope.

Fig. 24. - Detail of last Communion of St. Jerome.

MONUMENT OF GREGORY XIV *(22-opposite)* who was Pope for only ten months. The two small statues represent Faith and Wisdom.

Continuing, we remain spellbound while admiring the successful reproduction in mosaic of Domenichino's masterpiece, conserved in the Vatican Picture Gallery:

LAST COMMUNION OF ST. JEROME *(23)* (fig. 23-24). The Saintly Doctor, already old, pale and emaciated with penance and sufferings, supported by his pupils who with difficulty refrain from tears, strains himself to kneel in order to receive Holy Viaticum from the hands of Saint Efrem. With an expression of infinite sadness, the devout St. Paula

Fig. 25. - Monument of Gregory XVI

who had accompanied him on his pilgrimage to the Holy Land kisses the hand of her dying master. In the corner to the left, the grateful crouching lion seems to participate in the sorrow. Legend has it that, having been healed by the Saint, the lion became a defender of the monks; more likely, the lion may be a symbol of the noble temperament of the solitary Saint. Above, as if suspended in the sky, a group of graceful little angels look on edified and saddened by the moving scene. (fig. 23-24).

Turning to the right we are beneath one of the four domes *(24)* at the corners of the Greek Cross according to Michelangelo's plan which are 137.70 ft. high.

Fig. 26. - Monument of Benedict XIV

MONUMENT OF GREGORY XIV *(25 - to the right)* by Luigi Amici, was erected in 1855 by the Cardinals created during his Pontificate. At the sides of the Pope, who is giving his blessing, are the figures of Wisdom and Prudence, with the symbols of the mirror and the serpent. This Pope, when still Cardinal, was Prefect of the « Propaganda Fide » and the bas-relief of the sarcophagus represents his activities for the propagation of the Faith. The two beautiful columns of gray African marble were in a temple of the Roman Forum.

CHAPEL OF OUR LADY OF PERPETUAL SUCCOUR *(26)* called Gregorian because it was completed during the Pontificate of Gregory XIII (1572-1585) and below the altar lies the body of St. Gregory Nazianzen, Patriarch of Constantinople. [5]. Above the altar, rich in precious columns, mother-of-pearl, inlaid marble and bronze is an ancient image of our Lady from the Constantine Basilica which was placed here in 1580.

MONUMENT OF BENEDICT XIV *(27-further on the right)* (fig. 26) by Pietro Bracci. The popular and gentle Pope is shown blessing the people in the Jubilee Year, proclaimed by him in 1750. At the sides, two admirable statues. Wisdom, who looks towards the learned Pope with admiration; Detachment, who pushes away the riches offered her by a winged angel.

Fig. 27 - St. Basil celebrating Mass in the Basilica of Cesarea
(*Pietro Subleyras*)

ALTAR OF ST. BASIL *(28-opposite)* (fig. 27). Bishop of Cesarea and Doctor of the Greek Church. The picture in mosaic was done by Pier Leone Ghezzi from the original of Pietro Subleyras, which is in St. Maria degli Angeli. It represents the scene which took place in the Basilica of Cesarea of Cappadocia on the feast of the Epiphany 372. While the Saint was celebrating Mass before a devout congregation, the Emperor Valentius with his suite entered the Church to assist at the divine mysteries and to offer the gifts that he had brought. Lost in admiration at the devotion of the Saint, he was so overcome that he fainted.

A few steps in front (29) there opens up the vast impressive northern arm of the Greek Cross of Michelangelo.

Fig. 28. - St. Frances Xavier Cabrini (*E. Tadolini*)

Here, from December 8, 1869 to July 18, 1870, ging to the different reli- the Vatican Council was held, when, in the presence of about 700 Bishops, the dogma of the Infallibility of the Pope was proclaimed. In this transept solemn funerals are held, and every Sunday, during the Holy Mass at noon the Holy Gospel is explained.

Close to the walls, there are confessionals in which special confessors belongious orders hear the confessions of the faithful on Sundays and Feast Days.

Above the pillars we read the words addressed by Jesus to St. Peter: «*O Petre, dixisti tu es Christus filius Dei vivi. Ait Jesus, Beatus es Simon Bar Ionia quia Caro et Sanguis non revelavit tibi*». (« O Peter, Thou didst say: Thou Art Christ the Son of the Living God. Jesus said: Blessed art thou Simon, Bar Jonah, because flesh and blood did not reveal it to thee »).

The statues of the Holy Founders in this wing are:

On the right:

below: St. Cajetan of Thiene, C. Monaldi;

above: St. Frances Cabrini, E. Tadolini, (fig. 28);

below: St. Jerome Emiliani, P. Bracci;

above: St. Antide Touret, E. Quattrini.

below: St. Joseph Calasanctius, I. Spinazzi;

above: St. Bonfiglio, C. Aureli.

below: St. Bruno, M. Slodtz, (fig. 29);

above: St. Paul of the Cross, I. Iacometti;

On the left:

ALTAR OF ST. WENCES-LAUS, *(30-on the right)*, Bohemian King and Martyr killed by his impious brother Boleslaus. This mosaic was copied by Angelo Caroselli, Caravaggio's pupil.

ALTAR OF SAINTS PROCESSUS AND MARTINIANUS *(31-in the center)*. The mosaic by Cristofari in 1737, was taken from the picture by Jean de Boulogne. It represents the two Saints who, according to tradition, were the prison guards of St. Peter. They were converted and baptized by him, and later martyred in the presence of their parents. Their relics, formerly in the ancient Basilica, are preserved in the porphyry casket under the altar.

ALTAR OF ST. ERASMUS *(32-on the left)* mosaic by Cristofari, from the painting by Nicola Poussin. The Saint is barbarously tortured while a pagan priest pointing to an idol, tries to induce him to apostatize.

ALTAR OF S. PETER WALKING ON THE WATER *(33-on the left)*. Mosaic by

Fig. 29. - St. Bruno *(M. Slodtz)*

Cristofari, taken from the lively and bright canvas by Giovanni Lanfranco, 1727. The subject is the same as that by Giotto which we admired in the portico.

MAUSOLEUM OF CLEMENT XIII *(34-to the right)* (fig. 30-31), a master-piece by Canova, completed in 1792 after eight years of work. In this admirable group there are three main figures. Above, the Pope absorbed

Fig. 30. - Monument of Clement XIII *(Canova)*

in devout and fervid prayer. To the left, the noble and solemn personification of Religion with the motto in Hebrew on the forehead « The Lord is Holy « and on the belt « Doctrine and Truth ». To the right, the Spirit of Death, sad yet beautiful, holding the torch of life upside down and extinguished. At the base, two beautiful sculptured lions, one apparently sleeping and the other proudly stretched out, seem to be guarding the tomb. From the physical strength of the lions to the spiritual power of prayer, through religion which transforms death into true life is a sublime ascent towards God. This profound concept was impressed into the marble with the delicacy of the greek chisel by the main sculptor of neo-Classicism.

A few steps *(35)* ahead and we are under the second of the four corner Domes.

Fig. 31. - Detail of the Monument of Clement XIII

ALTAR OF ST. MICHAEL THE ARCHANGEL *(36-to the right)* (fig. 32) in which there is a copy in mosaic of the famous canvas by Guilo Reni which is in the capuchin church in Via Vittorio Veneto. The beauty of the face of the Archangel is such that the painter's contemporaries used to say: « Only by having been in Heaven could Guido have painted so beautiful a face ».

ALTAR OF ST. PETRONILLA *(37-to the left)* (fig. 33). It is the most richly coloured mosaic in the Basilica. In it Fabio Cristofari was able to preserve the character and style of Guercino's original which is kept

Fig. 32. - St. Michael Arcangel *(Guido Reni)*

Fig. 33. - St. Petronilla *(Guercino)*

Fig. 34.- Altar of the Chair and the Glory *(Bernini)*

SEGRETERIA DI STATO
DI SUA SANTITÀ

N° 327654

Dal Vaticano, li 22 Maggio 1954

Rev.mo Signore,

Non ho mancato di presentare al Santo Padre l'omaggio della Sua recente pubblicazione sulla Basilica di S.Pietro.

L'Augusto Pontefice, nel ringraziarLa vivamente di codesta testimonianza di sincera e profonda devozione, mi affida il venerato incarico di parteciparLe, a spirituale conforto, la Benedizione Apostolica, sicuro auspicio dei divini favori.

Mi è gradito aggiungere il mio ringraziamento per l'esemplare destinatomi, con squisita cortesia.

Profitto dell'incontro per confermarmi con sensi di distinta stima

della S.V.Rev.ma
dev.mo nel Signore

G.B.Montini

Rev.mo Signore
Sac. LUIGI GIUNTA

Città del Vaticano

Dear Father L. Giunta

I did not fail to present the Holy Father with the complimentary copy of your recent publication on the Basilica of St. Peter.

In expressing His warm thanks for the evidence of your sincere and profound devotion, the Supreme Pontiff has charged me to convey to you the spiritual comfort of the **Apostolic Blessing**, sure token of divine grace.

I want to add my thanks for the copy which you so courteously sent to me.

With sentiments of profound esteem, I am,

Very devotedly yours,
(Signed) G. B. Montini

in the Capitoline Gallery. Below: the Saint who did not wish to marry, obtains, by her prayers, the grace to die rather than marry the noble Flacco, before whose eyes, with their lost and almost incredulous expression, she is buried. Above: the Saint is received into Paradise by her heavenly bridegroom.

The relics of this martyr, discovered by Paul I in the Cemetery of Domitilla during the 8th Century, were placed in one of the two imperial rotundas which became the Chapel of the King of France, and were later placed under this Altar by Paul V.

The French from the Middle Ages were extremely devoted to this Saint and the sovereigns of France enriched with precious gifts this chapel, which was considered the National Chapel in the Constantine Basilica. On the Feast Day of this Saint, May 31, solemn Mass is celebrated at this Altar, in the presence of the Vatican Chapter and the French Ambassador to the Holy See, to whom liturgical honours are rendered.

Fig. 35. - Detail of the Altar of the Chair *(Bernini)*

THE ALTAR OF ST. PETER RAISING TABITHA TO LIFE *(38-further on the left)*. The artists of the Vatican School of mosaic, copied this in 1760 from the painting by Placido Costanzi.

MONUMENT OF CLEMENT X *(39-opposite)*. On the valuable marble urn on which the Pope is seated, in the act of blessing, there is sculptured the scene of the opening of the Holy Door in the Jubilee Year of 1675. The statues represent Mercy and Kindliness.

A Little further on, we find ourselves in the western arm of the Greek Cross of Michelangelo *(40)* and here we admire the gigantic masterpiece

Fig. 36. - Monument of Urban VIII *(Bernini)*

Fig. 37. - Monument of Paul III *(Della Porta)*

Fig. 38. - Detail of the monument of Paul III.

in marble, bronze and stucco, which covers the huge wall of the apse without hiding or altering the solemn architectural lines of Michelangelo.

ALTAR OF THE CHAIR AND THE GLORY by Bernini (41) (fig. 34-35). In the oratory of St. Hadrian, near the Basilica of St. Peter, was kept a wooden seat inlaid with ivory which, according to a continuous and uninterrupted tradition, was venerated as the authentic chair used by St. Peter in his Sacred Ministry. [6].

During the long history of this building, this venerable relic was moved on many occasions, until Alexander VII decided to put it in the central apse. He gave this task to Bernini, who responded to the Pope's request in the most grandiose and successful manner, expressing in his project a profound theological concept. With a flash of his boundless genius he raised the ancient relic high up among the clouds, closed as if in a precious jewel box, within a gilded bronze Chair.

48

Fig. 39. - The canopy and the Dome seen from below.

Fig. 40. - Confession and Chest containing Pallia.

From above the Holy Spirit, in the form of a Dove, surrounded by Angels hovering among dense clouds, sends down rays of Wisdom on the Chair of Peter, from which his successor spiritually guides the Christian world. The Western Church represented by Sts. Ambrose and Augustine (in front) and the Eastern by Sts. Athanasius and John Chrysostom (behind) in unity of Faith render homage to the Chair of the Vicar of Christ. At the sides of the chair, decorated with a gilt bas-relief of Jesus entrusting his flock to St. Peter, are two very beautiful Angels, while above there are two graceful Cherubs, holding a key in one hand, and supporting the tiara with the other.

The inscription over the pillars, in Greek and in Latin says: « O Shepherd of the Church feed all the Lambs and Sheep of Christ ». In order to form an idea of the size of this work, note that the dove (which looks quite normal) has a wingspan of 4½ feet. The white marble slabs commemorate the definition of the dogma of the Immaculate Conception, December 8, 1854, by Pius IX, and bear the names of the prelates at the solemn ceremony.

The statues of the Sts. Founders in this arm are:

To the right:	To the left:
below: St. Elia, A. Cornacchini	below: St. Benedict, A. Montauti
above: St. Francis de Sales, A. Favolini	above: St. Frances Romana, Galli;
below: St. Dominic, Le Gros	below: St. Francis of Assisi, P. Monaldi
above: St. Francis Caracciolo, Labourer.	above: St. A. M. de Liguori, P. Tenerani.

MAUSOLEUM OF URBAN VIII *(42-to the right)* (fig. 36), by Bernini who completed it in 1674. It shows the Pope raising his hand in blessing.

Statues of the finest marble symbolize Justice to the right, and Charity to the left. A gaunt skeleton traces the name of the Pope on a slab of marble, and here and there are bees of the Barberini coat of arms.

THE MONUMENT OF PAUL III *(43 - to the left)* (fig. 37-38), was done by Guglielmo della Porta under the direction of Michelangelo, 1576. It shows the noble figure of the Pope, who was 82 when he died, worn out by sorrow and old age, lifting his weary hand in blessing. At the base, separated by a striking mask found in the Farnese gardens, lie the figures of Justice portraying the Pope's sister Julia, (wife of Orsino Orsini) and Prudence with the features of the Pope's mother, Giovannella Gaetani.

Fig. 41. - Pius VI *(Canova)*

Here turning and proceeding to the Main Altar we find ourselves under the huge DOME, a wonder of the world and the most ambitious and daring architectural effort undertaken by man. Now we can admire this bold gigantic production of Michelangelo, called: « An abyss suspended above our heads » and appreciate still more the creative genius of this superb artist.

In order to be able to form a better idea of the grandeur and the harmonious proportions of this masterpiece, here are some figures. The height of the Dome from the ground to the Cross is 449.47 ft., the diameter 139.63 ft., the circumference 433.07 ft. The pillars which support it are 101.70 ft. high and the four arches have a diameter of 78.74 ft. The four medallions with the mosaics of the Evangelists and their relative symbols: St. John with the eagle; St. Luke with the calf; St. Matthew with the Angel; and St. Mark with the lion; all have a diameter of 27.55 ft.; the pen held by St. Mark is 8.20 ft. long. In the inscription overhead, the letters of which are 4.62 ft. high, we read: « *Tu es Petrus et super hanc petram aedificabo Ecclesiam meam et tibi dabo claves regni coelorum.* (Thou art Peter and upon this rock I will build my Church and to Thee I will give the keys of the Kingdom of Heaven).

51

Fig. 42. - The Martyrs Counterpane.

Great beams of light descend on the vast space below from the sixteen windows set between double Corinthian pillars with elegant frontspieces, alternately triangular and arched, while above, in a blaze of a thousand coloured lights, of stars and of gold, the vault, divided into sixteen sectors, converges on a lantern like skylight. It is decorated with ninety-six figures of Apostles Saints, Popes, Angels bearing instruments of the Passion, Cherubs and Seraphs, who bow in veneration towards the tomb of Peter while from above the Eternal Father appears to protect it.

Under the immense, luminous, dome, there stands another great work of the tireless Bernini: the bronze CANOPY *(44)* which impresses one not only by its hugeness, perfectly in proportion with the vast space in which it stands, but also by the originality of the work and the delicacy of its execution. fig. 39). It is 95.15 ft. high, weighs 610 quintals, was completed in 9 years, and was inaugurated on the feast of Sts. Peter and Paul, June 29, 1633.

From the center of the canopy, the HOLY Ghost in the form of a Dove seems to send down his rays on the PAPAL ALTAR *(45)*, made of a single massive block of marble. [7]. According to the custom of the early centuries, it is turned towards the people, and stands exactly over the tomb of the Apostle looking down on the very rich and magnificent CONFESSION *(46)* of *Maderno*. fig. 40). This is surrounded by a balustrade, from which horns jut inwards with nearly a hundred lamps always burning. Two flights of stairs go down to the level of the old Basilica where tradition has it that the little oratory of St. Anaclete stood. Here closed by a lovely gate, with gilt metal statues of St. Peter and St. Paul on each side, we find a niche nicely decorated with a ninth century mosaic. The floor of this niche, closed by a bronze grating with the coat of arms of Innocent X, is immediately over the tomb of the Prince of the Apostles. On it stands an artistic chest in which the pallia are kept. [8].

Before the tomb of St. Peter, depicted in marble by the sublime art of Canova, absorbed in the most fervent prayer kneels Pius VI *(47)*, who because of the sorrows he suffered and the humiliations he underwent, together with his death in exile, deserved to be buried near the first Pope of Rome. (fig. 41).

To cover the vast bareness of the immense pillars, the genius of Bernini succeeded in finding truly suitable expedients. Many notable relics were venerated in the Constantine Basilica, including the largest piece of the True Cross, donated by Pope Barberini, Veronica's Veil, venerated in Rome from time immemorial, the Lance that pierced Our Lord's side, presented by Sultan Baiazet to Pope Innocent VIII and the Head of St. Andrew given to Pope Pius II in 1460 by the King of Morea, Thomas Paleologus. The versatile artist adorned the sides

Fig. 43 - The Pillar with the statue of St. Longinus *(Bernini)*

of the four immense pillars facing the Confessional with balconies, huge statues and bas-reliefs relating to the above relics. Thus we can admire the statue of St. Helen *(48)*, by A. Bolgi, who, with noble and regal bearing holds the Cross and nails which she found in Jerusalem in the 4th century. [9]. From this balcony is exposed the martyrs counterpane (fig. 42); the Statue by Bernini St. Longinus *(49)* (fig. 43) who holds the lance in his right hand, while with his left hand outstretched seems to beg forgiveness.

In the pillar of St. Longinus, with a mosaic background resembling a drapery of antique brocade *(50)*, is the famous and popular Bronze Statue

Fig. 44. - Bronze Statue of St. Peter.

Fig. 45. - St. Leo the Great *(Algardi)*

OF ST. PETER (fig. 44) [10];
the statue of ST. ANDREW by
E. Duquesnoy, *(51)*, in an
ecstasy of love and faith embracing the Cross, the instru-
ment of his passion; and the
statue of VERONICA by F.
Moche *(52)* in an attitude
of breathless excitement as if
running to show the impression
which our Lord had left on the
towel with which he had wi-
ped his face. [11].

Having ended the visit to
what we can call the heart of
the Basilica, where the seed of
Christianity was sown and nur-
tured by the blood of the first
Apostle and thousands of other
martyrs and propagated throughout the world, we pass to
the right and come to the

MONUMENT OF ALEXAN-
DER VIII *(53)* erected in 1725
from a drawing by Arrigo de
Martino. On each side of the
bronze statue of the Pope, are
statues of Prudence and Religion. The bas-relief represents
the offering of gifts during the
canonization ceremony on October 16, 1690.

Fig. 46. - Altar of the Sacred Heart.

ALTAR OF ST. PETER CURING THE PARALITIC *(54-opposite)*.
The moving scene narrated in the third chapter of the Acts of the Apostles
was drawn here in 1760 by Ottaviano, life-like and in vivid colours. At the
door of the temple of Jerusalem, a cripple from birth begs alms of St. Peter
and St. John. St.Peter, moved with compassion, cures the cripple saying:
« Gold and silver I have not, but what I have I give thee, in the name of
Jesus of Nazareth arise and walk ».

We enter into the third square with one of the four corner domes *(55)*.

Fig. 47. - Mausoleum of Alexander VII

Fig. 48. - St. Thomas
(Camuccini)

ALTAR OF ST. LEO THE GREAT *(56 - to the right)* under which the Great Pope and Doctor of the Church is buried. (fig. 45). The grand marble tablet by Alessandro Algardi shows the Pope, aged and stern, assisted by Peter and Paul, repelling Attila, the scourge of God, thus saving Rome from destruction.

THE ALTAR OF THE COLUMN *(57-in front)*, dedicated to Our Lady, so called because the small image venerated there is painted on a piece of a marble column from the ancient Basilica. Beneath the altar there is a sarcophagous of the Third Century containing the relics of the Holy Popes Leo II, Leo III and Leo IV.

THE ALTAR OF THE SACRED HEART *(58-opposite).* The recent mosaic shows the scene of the appearance of the Sacred Heart to St. Margaret Mary Alacocque in the Chapel of Paray Le Monial. (fig. 46).

MAUSOLEUM OF ALEXANDER VII, *(59 - continuing to the right)* the most popular of the Basilica and last work of Bernini (fig. 47). It marks the end of the career of the great sculptor, painter and architect. Since it was necessary to place the monument above the door, the artist very successfully makes it part of the group. A skeleton of gilt bronze, as if coming out of the tomb, raising the heavy cover of Sicilian marble, shows the Pope absorbed in prayer, the hourglass marking the end of his days. The two figures behind represent Justice and Prudence, that in the front on the left, Charity presenting a child to the Pope, and, on the right, Truth placing her foot on the globe, blotting out England, which at that time was at variance with Rome because of the Anglican Reform.

We enter the impressive transept of St. Simon and St. Jude *(60)* corresponding to the one opposite of St. Processus and St. Martinianus. [12].

ALTAR OF ST. THOMAS *(61-to the right),* work of Camuccini. (fig. 48). The Apostle is portrayed at the moment when repentant of his incredulity, he touches the wound in

Fig. 49. Crucifixion of St. Peter *(G. Reni)*

59

the side of our Blessed Lord. Under the altar rests the body of Boniface IV, the Pope who consecrated the Pantheon to the Christian faith.

ALTAR OF SAINTS SIMON AND JUDE *(62-in center).* Beneath this altar are the bodies of the two Saints, and on each side of the altar in mosaic are two medallions. The mosaic of ST. JOSEPH was made recently in the mosaic studio of the Vatican.

THE CRUCIFIXION OF ST. PETER *(63-to the left).* The mosaic is a copy of the beautiful painting by Guido Reni. (fig. 49). Under the altar there are the mortal remains of Leo IX who died in 1054.

Fig. 50. - Ananias and Sapphira («*Pomarancio*»)

Fig. 51. - The Bronze cockerel.

The inscription above says: «*Dicit ter tibi, Petre, Jesus, diligis me? Cui ter o electe respondens ais Domine tu qui omnia nosti tu scis quia diligo Te*». (Jesus thrice said to thee, o Peter: Lovest thou me? To whom thrice o chosen one thou didst reply, Lord Thou knowest all things, Thou knowest that I Love Thee).

The statues of the founders in this transept are:

To the left:
Below: St. John of God, F. Valle
Above: St. M. E. Pellettieri, G. Niccolini
Below: St. Peter Nolasco, P. Campi
Above: St. Louise Marillac, A. Berti
 To the right:
Below: St. Juliana Falconieri, P. Campi
Above: St. Angela Merici, P. Galli
Below: St. Norbert, B. Cavaceppi
Above: St. William, G. Prinzi.

Fig. 52. - The Deposition *(Caravaggio)*

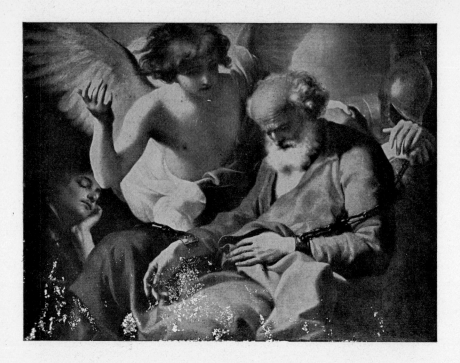

Fig. 53. - St. Peter Being freed from Prison *(A. Cavallucci)*

ALTAR OF ANANIAS AND SAPPHIRA *(64-continuing to the left)*, mosaic by Pietro Adami from the picture by Cristoforo Roncalli, who was called « Pomarancio ». (fig. 50). This picture represents the punishment of death inflicted by St. Peter on the couple Ananias and Sapphira because they had seriously lied to him.

MONUMENT OF PIUS VIII *(65-opposite)*. The famous neo-classical sculptor with an inspired religious feeling, represented the Pope kneeling, absorbed in prayer in his last hour. At his side, Peter and Paul seem to intercede for him, and above the Redeemer with open arms accepts his soul into the glory of the Saints.

SACRISTY AND TREASURY

We enter through the door under the monument of Pius VIII. *(66)*. In front is a statue in multicoloured marble of St. Andrew, executed in 1570; on the right, a tablet with the inscription of the names of the Popes buried in the Basilica, from St. Peter to Pius XI, 143 in all, 35 of whom are Saints. *(67)*.

Continuing along a wide corridor decorated by tomb stones, pillars and columns of coloured marbles with elegant white capitals, and later turning to the left, behind a glass partition, we find the Statue of Pope Pius VI *(68)*, who had the Sacristy built. The entrance to the Sacristy is opposite this statue. It is a large octagonal room with a dome which, including the cross, is 158 ft. high. *(69)*. In the middle of the beautiful floor is the artistic coat of arms of the Braschi Pope. The eight grooved columns which support the arches came from the Emperor Hadrian's villa at Tivoli. The bronze cockerel on top of the clock which used to be on a column of the ancient basilica symbolizes the betrayal of Peter and his sincere and bitter repentance. (fig. 51). In the background *(70)* we admire the beautiful recent mosaic copy of the Deposition by Caravaggio (fig. 52), which is in the Vatican Art Gallery. [13].

Through the left hand door we enter the Sacristy of the Canons *(71)* surrounded by cupboards of Brazilian mahogany, in each one of which

Fig. 54. - St. Peter converting his Prison Guards *(A. Cavallucci)*

is a drawer where the choir garments are kept. In the middle of the hall is a gilt metal bust of St. Peter on a column of Egyptian alabaster. The right hand door leads to the CHAPTER ROOM *(72)* where every 3rd Sunday the Canons meet to discuss matters regarding the Basilica, and where the Cardinals, Archbishops and Bishops of the whole world, after having visited the Tomb of St. Peter receive the testimonial of their « *visit ad limina* », signed by the Altar Canon.

Through the door in front we enter a CHAPEL. On the altar is an expressive painting by Francesco Penni portraying the Virgin, Child, St. Anne, and at the sides, the Apostles Peter and Paul. Above the door, ST. PETER BEING FREED FROM PRISON (fig. 53) and above the window, ST. PETER CONVERTING HIS PRISON GUARDS (fig. 54); both these picture are by A. Cavallucci.

Going back through the corridor we turn to the left to visit the treasury.

We pass through the SACRISTY OF THE BENECICIARIES *(74)*, which like that of the Canons is lined with cupboards. On the right hand door is the Deposition, inspired by a theme of Michelangelo, by L. Sabatini, an admirer and follower of the great master

Through the right hand door we enter another CHAPEL *(75)*. In it we admire the TABERNACLE OF DONATELLO, which was used for the Blessed Sacrament in the ancient Basilica and now serves as a frame for a lovely fresco of the Blessed Virgin, known as the Madonna of the Fever. The painting above the altar, Our Lord giving the keys to St. Peter is by Girolamo Muziano. On the door there is a scene from « Quo Vadis», and on the windows a picture of St. Andrew introducing his brother Peter to Jesus, both by A. Cavallucci. Continuing from the SACRISTY OF BENEFICED CLERICS *(76)* we observe a huge cupboard where lamps and candlesticks are kept. Beyond this cupboard we enter the Treasury *(77)*.

Fig. 55. - The Dalmatic (*called Charlemagne's*)

TREASURY

According to the *Liber Pontificalis*, the Treasury, originated with the numerous and precious gifts that the Emperor Constantine presented to the Basilica, just after it had been built. His example was followed by Theodoric, Justin, Clovis, Belisarius, Charlemagne and by many other Emperors and Kings, Cardinals and Popes, who left to the Basilica all the most precious possessions they had received during their lifetime. Many pilgrims of all centuries, from every nation, rich and poor, humble and great likewise contributed to this treasure.

Unfortunately so much wealth, given as a mark of love and devotion, had accumulated around the Tomb of Peter, that it would not pass unobserved by the various greedy and savage invaders of Rome, especially the Saracens in 846, and the Bourbons during the terrible sack of Rome in 1527. These looters did not leave even a chalice with which to celebrate Holy Mass. The French Republicans, besides carrying away all that had accumulated since the last invasion, forced Pius VI to turn the silver of the Basilica into coin in order to pay 20 millions demanded by the Treaty of Tolentino.

The present collection is formed by the gifts of the last century and by some objects that escaped the looters and have since been recovered. We shall cite only the most important of these.

I ROOM. A bronze group on a porphyry base, Jesus consigning the keys to St. Peter — sacred vestments completely embroidered in gold, presented by Cardinal Rampolla of Tindari in 1909 — a large Portuguese chalice in gilt silver — another in gold with diamonds, gift of Cardinal Henry, Catholics to Pius XI in 1932 — another in gold with diamonds, gift of Cardinal Henry, Duke of York — another in platinum, gift of Charles III, King of Spain to Pope Pius VI — Canon of the Mass on richly

Fig. 56. - One of the Silver Candlesticks *(Gentili da Faenza)*

65

Fig. 57. - One of the bronze Candlesticks
(Pollaiolo)

illuminated parchment — tiara of gilt silver and imitation stones which on great solemnities together with a rich red cape embroidered in gold is used to drape the bronze statue of St. Peter mentioned before.

II ROOM, called the Room of the Relics. We find the precious Vatican Cross of gilt silver and precious stones, gift of the Emperor Justin, which includes a large fragment of the True Cross and is shown in the Church on special occasions — another large fragment enclosed in a small gold frame, decorated with pearls and precious stones — to the left of the Holy Cross we see the image of Constantine who, according to tradition, used to carry this precious relic with him whenever he went to war — reliquaries of the Holy Lance, of the Holy Thorns, of the Blessed Virgin, of St. Blase, of St. Lucy, of St. Sebastian, of St. Venanzio and other Saints — Crown of twelve golden stars with precious diamonds, gift of the Catholic world in 1904 on the occasion of the 50th anniversary of the definition of the Dogma of the Immaculate Conception of Mary — monstrance of gold filigree — another of amber — another of rock crystal — another of silver called Berninian, because it faithfully reproduces the canopy of the great artist — in the middle, a valua-

Fig. 58. - Gregory the Great *(A. Sacchi)*

ble dalmatic, a byzantine work of the fourteenth century called Charlemagne's (fig. 55) — a great number of chalices, pyxes, patens, etc.

III ROOM. An altar cross with six silver candlesticks by Gentili
da Faenza, gift of Cardinal Alexander Farnese, (fig. 56) two very large
candlesticks of gilt bronze attributed to Pollaiolo, ordered by Julius II for
the tomb of Sixtus IV, (fig. 57), a Serbian icon of the thirteenth century
with the images of Sts. Peter and Paul — a very rich altar frontal embroidered in gold — plaster cast of the Pietà, from the original by Michelangelo.

Returning to the Basilica and turning to the right we find ourselves
beneath one of the four corner domes of Michelangelo *(78)*.

ALTAR OF ST. GREGORY THE GREAT *(79-to the right)*. (fig. 58)..
The scene in mosaic done in 1772 is from the painting by Andrea Sacchi.

Fig. 59. - The Transfiguration *(Raphael)*

Fig. 60. - Leo XI (*A. Algardi*)

Fig. 61. - Detail of the Monument of Leo XI.

taken from the life of the Holy Doctor written by Paolo Diacono. He had sent as a relic a piece of linen which had been on the tomb of the martyrs to a high personage, who unbelieving, brought it back to St. Gregory. Moved and repentant, he fell on his knees when he saw blood pouring forth from the white linen, where the Saint had pierced it with a dagger. The relics of the Holy Doctor are kept below the altar in an ancient sarcophagous. During his reign the Papacy reached the peak of its power as a result of which his name has been handed down with the addition of « Great ».

MONUMENT OF PIUS VII *(80 - to the left)* by the Danish sculptor Albert Thorwaldsen. The Pope with his emaciated face, seems to be showing signs of his sufferings in exile. He is shown seated in the act of blessing, between the winged genii of Time, with the hourglass, and of History who records deeds from the Pope's life. At the sides of the door, which leads to one of the choir organs, stand the statues of Wisdom, who meditates on the Bible, and Strength covered with a lion skin.

ALTAR OF THE TRANSFIGURATION *(81 - on the left)*. Mosaic by Monosilio, 1768, from the famous painting by Raphael which is in the Vatican Art Gallery (fig. 59). This work was ordered by Cardinal Giulio de' Medici in 1517 from the great painter, who because of his early death was unable to finish it and it was completed by his pupils Giulio Romano and Francesco Penni. Above: the gospel scene from the Transfiguration of Jesus on Mount

Fig. 62. - Innocent XI *(Pierre Monnot)*

Fig. 63. - The Chapel of the Choir.

Thabor; calm, solemn, divine ecstasy, celestial vision of light and glory. Below: an intensely dramatic scene of sorrow and hope, of despair and prayer, which contrasts with the heavenly serenity of the picture. The parents of a youth possessed by the devil, desolately take their son to the Apostles to intercede for his cure. In the center, an expressive figure of a woman (the Fornarina) anxiously invites and urges the followers of Christ to cure the unhappy child. But they, some with pity, others frightened, yet all trustful, point toward Christ above, the only source of life and salvation. This masterpiece of religious painting was put in the Sistine Chapel near the bier of the consummate artist who died at sunset, Good Friday, April 6, 1620, causing, according to Vasari, the hearts of all present to break with sorrow.

MONUMENT OF LEO XI *(82 - in the aisle to right)* by Algardi, 1650. (fig. 60-61). The Pope with the tiara and with his paternally expressive face, is seated on the sarcophagus on which is sculptured

Fig. 64. - Innocent VIII *(Pollaiolo)*

the abjuration of Protestantism by Henry IV in 1593. At the sides, are two very lovely statues: Liberality dropping coins and precious stones, and Strength with helmet, club and shield. Below these statues are two rose bushes denoting the brevity of his Pontificacy which lasted only twenty-seven days, brief as the flowering of a rose.

6

MONUMENT OF INNO-CENT XI *(83 - opposite)* by Pierre Monnot. (fig. 62). The Pope with a solemn expression and declamatory gesture, blesses with his right hand, and in his left he holds the tiara and keys. The figures at the sides represent Religion and Justice with the well known emblems, the cross, shield and sword. The bas-relief recalls the liberation of Vienna from the Turks through the intervention of the brave John Sobieski.

THE CHAPEL OF THE CHOIR *(84)* like that of the Blessed Sacrament, has an artistic gate at the entrance. (fig. 63).

The important architecture of the eight Corinthian pillars which support the four arches, all beatifully decorated — the walls and ceiling like golden embroidery — the golden medallions of scenes from the

Fig. 65-66. - S.S. Pius X

74

Fig. 67. - Funeral cenotaph of the last Stuarts *(Canova)*

Holy Scriptures — the carved choir stalls in dark walnut, designed by ber-nini — the elegant yet simple, frontispieces of the organs and choir — the large and beautiful mosaic of the Immaculate Virgin [14], who, midst a host of angels, receives the homage and veneration of St. Francis of Assisi, St. Anthony of Padua and St. John Crysostom, whose body is under this altar — all make this Chapel the most beautiful and the richest in the Basilica. [15].

MONUMENT OF INNOCENT VIII *(85 - next on the left)* by Antonio and Pietro Pollaiolo. (fig. 64). On the upper part is the Pope giving the blessing with his right hand, while in his left hand he holds a facsimile of the lance of Longinus. The bronze bas-reliefs at the sides represent the four Cardinal Virtues and those above the three Theological Virtues.

MONUMENT OF POPE PIUS X *(86 - opposite)* by Pier Enrico Astor-ri. (fig. 65-66). He died 1914, beatified 1951 and canonized 1954. The Pope is shown with a sad and paternal expression, his arms slightly raised as if to offer himself as a sacrifice to God to remove the scourge of war.

Fig. 68. - Maria Clementina Sobieski
(P. Bracci)

His sacrifice was accepted. His noble and gentle heart, unable to bear so much pain, ceased to beat and his blessed spirit sped to Heaven, as war spread throughout the world. The perfect lateral bas-reliefs refer to the most important events of his Pontificate: Communion of the Children, referring to the decree of the Great Pope by which he granted permission for children to receive Holy Communion as soon as they reached the age of reason; and, the Homage of the Wise Man to the Faith, referring to the condemnation of modernism.

ALTAR OF THE PRESENTATION OF THE CHILD MARY TO THE TEMPLE *(87)*, a mosaic taken from the picture by Francesco Romanelli. The Blessed Virgin, at a very young age, accompanied by Her parents Joachim and Anne, climbs the steps of the Temple where She is received by the High Priest. Below the Altar, object of ever growing veneration, lies the body of the Holy Pope, Pius X, of whom it can be said as of Christ, whom he so worthly represented on this earth: « poor and rich, meek and humble of heart ». For his simplicity, goodness and saintliness of life, he was declared Blessed on June 3, 1951 by Pope Pius XII, happily reigning.

MONUMENT OF BENEDICT XV *(88 - to the left)* who died in 1922, by Pietro Canonica.

FUNERAL CENOTAPH OF THE LAST STUARTS *(89)* by Antonio Canova, 1829, erected at the expense of George III, King of England. (fig. 67). Above are profiles of the pretenders to the English throne, James III and his sons Charles III and Henry IX. At the sides of the closed door are two genii holding torches of life, reversed and extinguished.

Fig. 69. - Baptism of Jesus Christ *(C. Maratta)*

MONUMENT OF MARIA CLEMENTINA SOBIESKI *(90 - opposite)* by Pietro Bracci (fig. 68). Charity, with an inspired face, is shown seated on a large cover of alabaster together with an angel carrying a portrait of the Queen, who died in Rome in 1735. Below are two graceful cherubs placing the royal emblems, the sceptre and the crown, on a cushion.

CHAPEL OF THE BAPTISTRY. *(91).* The three mosaics in this chapel are among the best in the Basilica. The one in front; Baptism of Christ in the River Jordan, is a copy from Carlo Maratta, done in 1722 (fig. 69). It has a great scenic effect and is outstanding for its conception and distribution of colours (note the feet of Christ which can be seen in the waters of the River). On the left: St. Peter preparing Cornelius, Roman Centurion, for his Baptism, from a picture by Andrea Procassini. On the right: The same Apostle baptizing his guards, Processus and Martinianus, with the water which springs miraculously from the Mamertime Prison where he had been held. This picture is by Passeri. In the middle: The Baptismal font made from a large basin of red porphyry, which may have originally come from some sumptuous Roman sarcophagus, later used as a cover for the casket of Otto II. The cover is by Carlo Fontana.

We have paid a quick visit to the Basilica of St. Peter and admired the materpieces which enrich it. The grandeur and beauty of this immense « Cathedral of Humanity » stands out clear to the visitor. Here everything reveals itself as grand, splendid and triumphant. Here, rather than meditating on Christ on Calvary and his sufferings, we are led to ecstacy over the sublime vision of Christ on Thabor. Here, is the apotheosis of Faith, the firmness of Hope, the triumph of Charity.

THE ASCENT TO THE DOME

The entrance is under the Monument of Maria Clementina Sobieski *(90)*, in the passage between the first and second Chapels on the left. We can go up to the flat roof by lift or by a spiral staircase of 142 steps. Along the walls are numerous memorial tablets of the ancient ceremonies of the opening of the Holy Door, and of ascents made by kings and eminent personages.

From the roof of the basilica we are impressed by the wastness and daring of the central dome which is surrounded by twelve smaller domes. (fig. 70). A double staircase leads into a large corridor which comes to an

Fig. 70. - The Dome *(Michelangelo)*

end at the first internal circular gallery of the dome. We are at a height of 83 meters, and looking down we are surprised and frightened by the huge space, where everything seems drawn in miniature, and the most colossal monuments, such as the Canopy and Chair by Bernini, appear so small; while gazing upwards we remain spellbound admiring the wonderful colours of the mosaics which portray the figures of the Holy Popes, and higher up the Redeemer, the Blessed Virgin, Saint John the Baptist and the twelve Apostles, then higher still the angels with the instruments of the Passion of Jesus Christ, and finally the Cherubs and Seraphs who surround the figure of the Eternal Father on the Lantern dome. (fig. 71).

Ascending by a narrow staircase we reach the gallery where the view, unique in the world, takes in at a single glance the history of thirty centuries.

Looking from right to left, we see the Apostolic Palaces, with the various impressive courtyards, that of the « Pappagalli » (Parrots) — of the guards — of St. Damasus, with the stained glass windows of Raphael's loggias — of the Belvedere — of the Library — of « Pigna » with the monumental niche by Bramante and the famous gilt bronze pine cone — the Governor's Palace — the railway — the Mosaic studio — the Leonine Walls — the Observatory and radio station — the reproduction of the Grotto of Lourdes, where the Holy Father walks in the gardens. In the background Monte Mario — on the left the Janiculum Hill with the equestrian statues of Garibaldi and Anita, and then St. Paul's and beyond, when the weather is good, the sea. Then, towards the East, Rome, the eternal city of the Caesars within our view, the Tiber meandering tortuously dividing the city, and uniting it again with the various bridges, Sisto, Umberto, Sant'Angelo, Vittorio Emanuele, Cavour, etc... The Austere mausoleum of Castel Sant'Angelo, and the imposing Palace of Justice, the ancient dome of the Pantheon, the sumptuous monument of Victor Emmanuel, the the classical palaces, Farnese, Quirinal — the Campidoglio — the ancient Colosseum and the ruins of the Imperial Forum of the Terme — the Palatine, with the green hills rich in glorious historical memories — the splendid fountains — the artistic churches — the innumerable domes — bell towers, silent and eloquent witnesses of Roman and Christian greatness.

SACRED GROTTOES

Sangallo, in his reform of Bramante's plan, raised the floor of the new Basilica by 9.56 ft., thus creating an intermediary space, which is known as the Crypt of St. Peter's or the Holy Vatican Grottoes. They are formed by a large rectangular room with a low ceiling supported by pillars, which divide it into three aisles extending from the Confession to the Chapel of the Blessed Sacrament. The entrance for priests celebrating Holy Mass on the Tomb of the Prince of the Apostles, is through a small door under the statue of St. Andrew; whereas that for the visitors is in front of the staircase of the Sacristy, which is reached through the Arch of the Bells, on the right, coming out of the Church. (92)

Fig. 71. - The Dome seen from the first Internal Gallery.

Fig. 72. - Interior of the Sacred Grottoes

At the entrance there are two small statues of St. Peter and St. Paul, worn out by time, which originally decorated the portico of the ancient Basilica. In the two following halls: sarcophagi, fragments of inscriptions and balustrades: in the third hall to the right, a staircase flanked by pieces of wall from the Constantine Basilica, which leads into the excavations which can be visited only with the permission from the office of the «Rev. Fabbrica».

These excavations, started by a wise project of the present Pope, Pius XII at the beginning of his Pontificate, have brought to light the necropolis which stood beyond the Northern end of Nero's Circus, where many Christians were buried, among whom, as we have already said, was St. Peter.

Among the many discoveries made, we note: funeral chapels, some of them of great archeological interest, such as the family chapels of the Cetenni, the Valeri, the Tulli, the Marci; Christian tombs with symbols and expressions already used among the first followers of Jesus Christ, such as the doves, olive branches, palms; very valuable sarcophagi from the Second and Third Centuries; ancient coins, etc.

Constantine wanted his Basilica to be built on the precise spot where St. Peter was buried and where Anacletus had built his Oratory. So, this area (certainly not the most suitable for the stability of the big building) was covered with carth, and here, the foundations were laid, evident sign that here was the tomb of the Prince of Apostles.

On the left, through a door, we enter three other halls: in the first, fragments of mosaics from the ancient temple; in the second, Papal tombs and more fragment of inscriptions and monuments; in the third, the artistic bronze monument, masterpiece of Pollaiolo, to Sixtus IV (Della Rovere), great patron of the arts and famous for the construction of the Sistine Chapel.

Returning, by means of six steps, we enter into the impressive large room corresponding to the Basilica (fig. 72). Beginning the visit towards the left, we find: Sarcophagus of Callistus III (1455-1458) — of Pius III (who reigned only for twentysix days, from September 22 to October 18, 1503) — the tomb of Hadrian IV (only English Pope, 1154-1159) — ancient Christian sarcophagus of Gregory V (996-999), — tomb of Otto II, who died in Rome in 983 — altar with ancient mosaic: « The Saviour between the Apostles Peter and Paul.

Continuing the visit: old statue of St. Peter. Further in front Altar to the Blessed Virgin, a fresco by Lippo Memmi — to the right of this, tomb of Nicholas III (1277-1280) — to the left tomb of Boniface VIII (1294-1303. In front, the tomb of Nicholas V (1447-1455) — of Innocent VII (1404-1406) and of Julius III (1550-1555).

On the left, among the many sarcophagi we admire that of Anicius Probus and Junius Bassus with beautiful episodes from the life of St. Peter. (fig. 73).

Continuing the visit: a medieval altar with sculpture from the School of Donatello — then the tomb of Marcel II — tomb of Innocent IX, — to the left, tomb of Benedict XV (1914-1922); further in front to the right, tomb of Christine of Sweden, to the left, Carola, wife of Ludovico of Savoy.

Fig. 73. - Sarcophagus of Junius Bassus.

Fig. 74. - Chapel of St. Peter

Little further to he right, tomb of John XXIII. In the centre, at the end of the central nave, altar of Christ the King with medallions in marble of the four Evangelists; to the right, altar of the Virgin with Child and with St. Peter and St. Paul; to the left of this, tomb of Pius VI (1775-1799).

Turning to the right in a room at a lower level, we find the monument of Paul II (1464-1471) of Mino, Dalmata and others.

Going through the passage around the Confession we arrive at the Chapel of St. Peter, whose altar, rich in lapis-lazuli, malachite and porphyry is placed over the tomb of the Apostle. In front, tomb of Pius XII (fig. 74) continuing along this corridor, we come on the right to the Chapel of the Madonna of the «Bocciata», which takes its name, according to tradition, from the fact that an evil person struck this image (which stood in the vestibule of the ancient Basilica) with a bowl, and blood poured forth from the cheeks of the Virgin.

Then comes the Chapel of the Madonna of women in childbirth; to the right, we enter into the Church behind the statue of St. Andrew; to the left, the Altar of the Suffering Christ.

Continuing, to the left, the tomb of Pius XI (1922-1939); of Cardinal Merry Del Val, Secretary of State of S.S. Pius X; of the Stuarts, pretender to the English throne; of Innocent XIII (1721-1724); of Urban VI 1378-1379) and then we find ourselves at the exit. But before leaving this mystic subdued light, beside the tomb of the First Apostle, where we feel closer to God, let us profess our glorious Faith, that Faith in Christ, which reddened these sacred slopes with the blood of the Martyrs; let us pray that all the souls of this troubled world, may hearken to the heart rending « Sitio », of the dying Redeemer, and be united in one flock under one Shepherd, The Successor of Peter.

84

NOTES

[1] The four modern memorial stones announce in eight languages the privilege which the Basilica enjoys and which every Christian should remember, namely a plenary Indulgence, applicable also to the dead, to be gained as often *(toties quoties)* as a person in the State of Grace visits the Church and recites 6 our Fathers 6 Hail Marys and 6 Glorys according to the intentions of the Holy Father. Confession and Communion can be made in any church or oratory.

[2] This altar consecrated by Pope Benedict XIII, February 19, 1727, was declared a privileged altar and as such confirmed by Pope Benedict XIV, December 22, 1749. The other Privileged Altars in the Basilica are: that of the Choir Chapel and that of St. Peter's Tomb, according to the Papal Brief on Privileged Altars: « Through the autority transmitted to us we grant that every time Mass is said on this altar for the repose of a faithful departed soul, the same soul gains from the inexaustible treasury of the merits of Our Lord, Our Lady, of Sts. Peter and Paul and all the Saints, release from Purgatory ».

[3] Many of these relics, enclosed in beautiful reliquaries, are exposed on the Papal Altar on the Fridays of Lent, during the month of March, on Saturday of Quarter Tense, Passion Sunday and November 18, feast of the Consecration, and on Easter Monday after Vespers on the balcony over the statue of St. Helen.

[4] Masses are celebrated frequently in this chapel. A priest vested in surplice and stole is always present to give Communion to the faithful who request it.

[5] This is one of the seven altars in the Basilica « *Unum ex septem* ». The seven altars are: Our Lady of Succour; the Altar of the Column; Sts. Processus and Martinianus; St. Michael the Archangel; St. Petronilla; Sts. Simon and Jude and St. Gregory. A partial indulgence of 7 years may be gained by visiting the « seven altars » and praying to the respective Titular Saint. A plenary indulgence may be gained on the feast of the Titular Saint, on the usual conditions of Confession and Communion, by praying at the altar for the intentions of the Holy Father. A plenary indulgence is also granted to those who visit the « seven altars » on the usual conditions mentioned above..

[6] The Chair of St. Peter has always been the object of profound veneration. There was an altar dedicated to it in the ancient Basilica and we know from St. Leo the Great that the Converts, immediately after their Baptism, went there to pay homage. On January 18, feast of St. Peter's Chair at Rome and February 22 at Antioch, it was carried in solemn procession by the Canons to the Choir Chapel for the Office. The veneration of this Holy Chair was such that St. Gregory the Great included, among the relics sent to Queen Teodolinda, a cruet of oil that burned before it: « From the oil of the Seat where St. Peter first sat ». Stefano Piale has left us a front and side view which are kept in the Chapter Room.

[7] So called because the Holy Father alone can say Mass here. It is only by special concession of the Holy Father that some one else may celebrate here. On Holy Thursday, after Tenebrae, the altar is washed with wine and water by the Canon Hebdomadarian and 6 assistants, after this the Cardinal Archipriest, followed by the Chapter and clergy present, dries it with the « aspergillo » and, lastly, the Hebdomadarian and the assistants complete the drying with towels while the Canons recite psalm 21. This ancient custom recalls our Lord's humility in washing the feet of the Apostles, or the blood and water that came from Our Lord's side, Symbols of Baptism and Eucharist.

[8] The pallia are strips of white wool, about two inches wide, with 5 black silk crosses. The wool comes from the lambs blessed on the feast of St. Agnes. The Pope blesses the pallia after the first Vespers of the feast of St. Peter, and they are kept in the afore-mentioned chest. They are given to Patriarchs and Archbishops as a sign of their jurisdiction and of their union with the Holy See. It is worn over the chasuble at Pontifical High Mass also by His Holiness.

[9] From this balcony, minor relics are exposed on Easter Monday at Vespers: on the feast of St. Andrew, the head of the Apostle is exposed. The martyrs Counterpane is exposed on Ascension Thursday and replaced for the feast of St. Peter in Chains. This Counterpane contains a sheet, in which, according to tradition, the bodies of the martyrs were wrapped for burial.

[10] The right foot of St. Peter is well worn with the kisses of millions of faithful of every century. On the feast of the Apostle, June 29, the people of Rome show their love and veneration for the great yet humble fisherman of Galilee, by kissing the foot of the statue. On this day and other big feasts, a red cope embroidered with gold and a tiara are placed on it.

[11] From this balcony one of the Canons blesses the people with the above-mentioned relics on the 2d Sunday after Epiphany; on Whitmonday when the Archiconfraternit of the Holy Ghost comes to the Basilica; on Ember Saturdays in Lent; Passion Sunday after the Procession; on Wednesday of Holy Week after tenebrae; on Holy Thursday and Good Friday, morning and evening after the services; on Holy Saturday after High Mass; on Easter Monday after Vespers; on May 3, feast of the Finding of the Holy Cross after Mass and after Vespers; and, on November 18, feast of the Dedication of the Basilica, after Mass and Vespers. This privilege belongs to the Canons of St. Peter's.

[12] In this transept, there are twelve Confessionals, where the ordinary confessors of the order of Friars Minor Conventual hear confessions in the chief European languages.
Under the statue of St. Juliana Falconieri, on the afternoon of Good Friday, and Holy Thursday there is placed a walnut chair which ordinarily stands by the altar of the Sacred Heart. The Cardinal Penitentiary on these days, during the singing of Tenebrae touches the heads of those who kneel at his feet. The confessors do the same whenever the faithful request it. This ceremony has its

origin in the gesture by which, according to the Roman Law, the slave was freed. The indulgence granted for this was raised to 300 days by Pope Pius XII happily reigning on the ocasion of his priestly Jubilee, when the confessors touch the heads of those in the state of grace, and to 7 years when the Cardinal Penitentiary does the same on Holy Thursday and Good Friday.

[13] From seven in the morning until one o'clock there is always a priest here who can be contacted by anyone wishing to celebrate Holy Masses in the Basilica, or for any other information concerning the administration of the Sacraments or religious functions.

[14] This image was solemnly crowned, immediately after the definition of the dogma of the Immaculate Conception, by Pius IX, December 8, 1854, in the presence of the Cardinals and Bishops in Rome. This occasion is commemorated on a stone.

[15] Here on Feast days and on certain other occasions, the Vatican Clergy consisting of the Canons, Beneficiaries and beneficied clerics presided over by His Eminence, the most Reverend Archpriest of the Basilica, celebrate the Divine Office assisted by the singers of the Julian Chapel founded in 1512 by Pope Julius II. Pier Luigi da Palestrian was Choir Master of this Chapel for twenty-eight years.

INDEX

The Tomb of St. Peter . . . . , . . Pag. 5

The Constantine Basilica . . . . . . » 6

History of the new Basilica . . . . . . » 8

A visit to the Basilica . . . . » 13

Sacristy and Treasury . . . . » 63

The ascent to the Dome . . . . » 77

Sacred Grottoes . . . . » 79

Per ordinazioni rivolgersi:

L. GIUNTA - Via Annéo Lucano, 62 - Roma - Tel. 348640

CHICCA - TIVOLI